Body Tapestries

Body Tapestries

S. D. Lishan

Dream Horse Press
California

Library of Congress Cataloging-in-Publication Data:

Lishan, S. D.
        Body Tapestries

                p.   cm

                ISBN 0-9777182-1-2
                1. Poetry

10 9 8 7 6 5 4 3 2 1

First Edition

Table of Contents

"His father looked at him in amazement, 'How would you know what the sparrows are saying?'

'My teacher taught me the languages of the various animals.'"

—from an Italian folktale, retold by Italo Calvino

With gratitude to my teachers over these many years, both in and out of the classroom: Kathy Fagan, John Frisius, Terry Hermsen, Merrill Lishan, Nancy Johnson, Philip Levine, William ("Mac") MacDuff, Neal ("Pete") Peterson, Peter Sears, Amy Shuman, and Mark Strand.

And, as always, most deeply, for Lynda, the weaver of my heart.

Introductory Notes

In 1986 the 1st voice arrived.

I'm a fiend in high school, like dead sky, man.

The voice of Monkey Boy. Lonely high school kid, he
who has a deep crush on a girl named Felisha. He
has an affair with a kid named Angel, in part because
he wants to, in part because he can't have Felisha.
Monkey Boy commits suicide when he sees Felisha
being "intimate" with other boys after a football game.
Once dead, he learns to be an angel, kissing "the cut
wrists and the burns" of those who have survived their
attempts to kill themselves. He touches their flesh. He
feels their lips upon his own.

And then other voices came.

The Duchess of Moisture. Her anger blooms, erupts
into a flower of violence upon the world she inhabits.
Her anger is a motive force that propels many of the
narrative threads in the sequence, twists them about,
frays them, rearranges them.

Which is to say,
and so on.
Which is to say,
and sew on.

The Duchess dotes on a character named Moonlight, and he for her, seemingly. But he is a coward, a cad. He professes love for the Duchess, then leaves her for another, The Princess Waterfall, and then, when the Duchess's troops pursue him, he in turn leaves the Princess to be guarded by the Woodcutter Turned Into A Tree, until his return. But, as might be expected from a coward, a cad, he never returns, ending up instead at the edge of the universe, writing postcards home, living on a cusp of solitude and loneliness.

Which is to say…

Meanwhile, Princess Waterfall has a child by him, a daughter, Moonlit Lake, who is murdered by the Duchess's troops. Because longing and grief can be read in many ways, and flows down many different paths, the poems in her voice can be read both across and down in a sort of columnar way. Like Lot's wife turned into a pillar of salt.

And sew on.

These narratives have been woven into silken tapestries by Caterpillar, a faithful recorder (she who even records the moment of her death, *Thus I was*).

And so in the weave of we've, the characters came.

The Leech Oracle, who predicts what will happen to these tapestries.

Turtle, who, when the Duchess of Moisture's anger erupts, escorts Caterpillar through the sea on her shell to seek help from the Dolphin Queen. They arrive at her citadel too late.

Graybeard worm, who escapes from being shoveled into the maws of the "scabied brood" of the Duchess's ally, the Empress Waterfowl, she who has presence but no voice in these proceedings. Old Graybeard, crafty old thing, escapes to tell his tale, which is then repeated by a younger worm, but, though the sounds are the same, as in a game of telephone, the words come out differently.

And others. Which is to say, the world presented itself slowly.

In pieces.

But how should one take these funny named fairytale-like characters? Ironically? Archetypically? As the Woodcutter Turned Into A Tree says, *To everything, yes.*

Coinciding/colliding/interweaving, the narratives start, the narratives stop, the narratives pick up again, are embellished, are responded to by different characters, are transformed, transmuted, translated, even

as they are transmitted. Within the larger frame of
narrative, there are sub-narratives that trail off, only
to be picked up again later in the sequence. There
are various voices, often within the same poem, and
differing layers of intertextualities. The Duchess of
Moisture, for example, has written an autobiography
that co-exists within the sequence as a sort of shadow
text. A reader/listener will construct these voices in
different ways, is invited to construct these voices in
different ways.

And sew on. The sequence attempts to thrive off
the scintillates, the energy produced when a poem
approaches a recognizable form and then veers away
from it, the sonnets intentionally becoming scarred
and splintered in the process.

The fact that the sequence is entitled *Body Tapestries*
is meant to suggest that the tapestries are within us,
a mapping of sorts of some of the [un?]common,
interior spaces that we share.

For if poetry is a record, can it be with the emphasis
on *cord*, which sounds like *chord*, as in music or a line
joining two points on a curve, which is an attempt
to tie together, to connect, and on *re*, to connect
together again. And again. And then again.

The Breeze-Fluttered Tapestry: April

"Inward"; "Cold!" Such is the pared speech of blossoms
In their bent attitude of coyness, or of shame;
As April rain congeals to snow, like lost suns
The daffodils curl on themselves, and I, in the same
Bowed speech, remember that far off summer
When you were gone, that night at Sweet Springs,
Where I wandered under the tide-swelled star-
Light that cantilevered past the water rings,
Past the frog songs, past the caterpillar
Spinning her silks into the fog-filtered moonlight —
These breeze-fluttered tapestries of my years —
So they seemed that eucalyptus-scented night
As the dew fell, and the caterpillar's silks glistened;
"Come," they shone, "Begin here; closer; listen…"

Part One:
Tales Of Twilit Seasons
(The Tapestries Of Power)

Each In Their Turn: Forest Creatures At Twilight

"Tonight I hear the caves the gulls call sea,"
   Frog, in his heart, flames, where spring's breath brushes
   The pond's edge, and, floating moonlit like sighs,
   The algae lean into the windblown rushes;

Then the tide moves; "Don't go," sings the owl;
                                       "Damn the king-
   Fisher who rattles his throat at me; in this place
   I need sleep," sobs possum, "and forgetting…"
"In our village it is the blue phases

   Of dusk we revile," the daisies curl;
"Under the storms the world grows white, into a lovely
   Radiance I cannot find," so unfurls
   The heron who glides over the bay;
                         "And I,"

   Rasps mantis, "make leaf cities tremble at my will,
   But I'm remembered by nothing; is my shadow so evil?"

The Antagonists: The Duchess Of Moisture, The Empress Of Waterfowl

The Duchess of Moisture streamed from her castle;
Deep in her mitered soul she was enraged;
She arranged her forces for the battle;
It was a drear morning; in the village,
By the tall volcano, near the rivers,
And in our houses, her anger began;
Her sea witches were sent to claim us; the oars
They rowed with were golden; far inland
My muscles were tired; buoyed by the dead horses,
The Empress of Waterfowl, her purple
Pennant raised, cried out to the marshes,
To the curlews and sheldrakes, the supple
Formations of swans; the moon showed what was left;
No quality of language could spell our grief.

When The Grape Became Purple: The Aged Genii Recalls The War Of His Kind Against The Moisture Duchess

Then the mother genii's belly opened;

Then, disgorging their arrows and their armor,

Her babies, slithering like cobras, were siphoned

Into the light; the Duchess began her war;

Her clouds arced over us, like dinner plates,

Exploded, and the shards massed into black skeletons;

They climbed towards us over the walls of burial plots;

Then her hot rain burst into our scalded bones,

And we climbed onto wolves and rode away, cowards;

It was autumn when finally we felt safe;

The grapes were shiny and ripe, unbled, uncolored

Still by their shame of us; we slid their soft

Skins back, like the shut eyelids of dreamers, and in

We curled, stunned, waiting… for the world to be naive again.

Why We Sometimes Don't Say Anything In Dreams: Monkey Boy

I'm a fiend in high school, like dead-sky, man;

Like in the shake line my hair gathers like fur;

Like when I climb the bleachers during gym
And hooch for hours, Coach says, "Save it for
Friday";

       like things swim in front of my eyes
(Like when a Harley starts I think, "lion");

Like that ROTC kid kicks me, says, "Say yes
Sir, YES SIR!"
          Like eat my heart for dinner, man;

Like I give Felisha grubs in study hall;

Like my dick is crawling with larval flies;

Like trees trees trees they're fucking beautiful;

Like there's this thing in my head and there's wires;

Like Doctor Kramer says, "Sit back, try not
To breathe," so I don't, and it's like. . . , so I don't.

Tapestry Of Blossoming Senses: A Notation Of Spring While Watching Two Bicyclists Stop By A Pond

Sunlight ajar like in adore, silence

Tipped toads past the blue sky's skinned coolness, the reels

Of rippled bright; untied, flecks of unfenced

Soar scent above pond's edge; one feels like the peals

Of a church bell; cloud-midriffs huff-shuffle

Down wind, unsettled, sun-nicked, as the wasps

Purr "hold the day," like curled-up coeurs shush full

Of sting-song rinsed by the violet's violet clasps;

Petal soft voices now; nearby lies

Breeze-torqued human touch, heart-sparkled,

Like fist fulls of mint at a well spring; idled

Fog unclumps; after these two, in love, lilies

Bloom, and the first fireflies have suckled

Against evening, after the last bees have wild.

Where Lullabies Go: The Pond On An Early Winter Evening

"Ooh la la," the mud purrs; "ooh lullay,"
Water bubbles; "turtle-turtle-skin-like-tissue-
Shell-on-fire," the frogs taunt;

                                       their lovely
Hearts claimed by fog, leaves cackle, "Miss you…"

As they disappear;

                    Voice of the Night cries,
"Waterbugs, boil in rage, the night is long,
The night…";

              fish eye the stars with misgivings, "Fish eyes,
Fish eyes, come away," so goes their song;

And so winter came, climbing scraggly treetops,
Lit by the gray, streaked wind;

                    up there
In the trees egrets wish for the moon to stop,
And then to slither down, down, further…;

"Little Whitefeather in the stars so bright,"
They kiss their children, "sleep, sleep, this early winter night."

The Duchess Of Moisture Reads To Me
From Her Autobiography: Her Early Years

Insect who damns me with woman's weaving, you,
Why should I not be defined by my memories; listen:

"I was suckled where no sea bloomed, my only view
A prairie bleached, monotonous as moonlight; but when
The mercuries in my begetters' blood burned
And drove them to move, we moved; I remember
The distant salt scent; then, closer, as we turned
The curve of the hills, the sea unfolded; November
Squalls curtained the horizon; the cold
Drizzle and tingle of the salt sea loathed
What I was, what I would jettison behind; that I could
Give praise to cunning and flaming hate that seals the oath
To my besieged sea love; when I acquired power,
I vowed to bring the leveling sea there, then there…, then here."

Monkey Boy's In-Class English Theme: Angel And A Desperado Heart

It's like, my brain explodes in this page whiteness,
So like I turn in: "Hunters in bungalow walls, in vice
Principal's hassle down passless hallways; 'Worthless,'
He points at me, this power man in lullaby voice…

And then there's Coach; Coach! Aargh! Hate him!

Lunch time — wolf bark-lockers slam; 'He gets crazier';
Felisha points from her slum of friends — now home
Is Angel sucking me off in his Olds cruiser;
It's like I disappear, like in, in a forest:

Moonlit sounds — hoot owl, wind, mole,
Touch of waterfall mist; finally, rest…

Now Coach and narcs — 'Bang!' — banging on the window;
Wolves bark from the halls of trees; I think, 'Hide!'
Fences everywhere, bells, bloody clangs in my head."

How, In The Season's First Snowfall, Frog Came To Leave His Pond In Quest Of The Sea

Voices like a wounded language — like pins
Of ice in trees they pricked into his skull
As the pond's edge froze; that sunset, the bay's thin
Necklace of tides shimmered, until snow fell;
It whipped into him; it made our bones ache;

And as I listened, each voice seemed as lost:

". . . It begins —   ". . . There is a sound   ". . .The sea makes
Like a scythe that cuts   That whispers   Her healing loosened
From the swath   That empties   From a shell of sighs
That is her flesh   Like waterfalls   Surrendering. . ."
To remake us. . ."   It begins. . . "

                                    Frog heard the voices rise
Like mists of breath on cold days surrounding
him, as tides fingered the marsh grass like a lyre,
As he set out to make the sea his lover.

Angel's Passion: Angel And Monkey Boy Park Off The Deep Woods Road

How does that feel? And that? And this? Look, gusts
Of leaves swirling in a trance, man — heart flutters;

Hey, Pretty Boy, loll on me; like it's midnight, ghosts
Rise off the hot car hood; these are the queer words
I whisper, man — "Pretty, Pretty Boy"; you see,
With my tongue and my hands, I can be a king
For you, like heart's mirror, like truth — look at me;
Don't treat me like the Other— look!

                               That stinking
Girl's in your thoughts; I can see her fantasy moves,
But you'd be wingtip borne, an impresario queen
With me, you, who has forgotten the scent of my love;

These Felisha thoughts — why can't you let me wean
Them from you? In my heart you're the moon that pulls;
I'm the tide and you draw me to you, suckled, full.

Where I Comment Upon The Main Action In These Tapestries So Far

The Duchess of Moisture's fortunes grew rosier,

After the squadrons of shadows were gassed,

When the commands came to wear her cough forever,

When her spacecraft landed, when its blackness

Leeched out light, when the Duchess of our disease

Waved her flag and her black eyes glittered through portholes;

When the captains of barracudas, our countries

Secured now, came in from their patrols;

When, "Fraulein Moisture," they said, "we have taken care

Of Moonlight, the enemy of your people";

When we fought back with rocks and received these scars;

Yes, back then we had a song; its words were simple;

They made us believe that one forgets pain,

That the gift in afterwards is that sweetness remains.

Part Two:
Moonlit Tales
(The Tapestries Of Love)

At The Worm's Campfire:
The Graybeard's Story

To the Apricot City, the Leprechauns bear their dead —
Yes, they die, and sweeter than apples they are;
I've tasted their thin nerves that lead to the head,
To their eyes, and the sweet plumage of aery hair,
The brain's velvet glove; that night they marched,
And I, famished, followed, when the Empress of Waterfowl
Appeared, hissing, her feral back arched;
They asked her to let them pass, and her wings whirled
Around them, like a black hurricane, in answer;
She bore us to her nest (I, the fool,
Was a captive, too) on her sea-cliff mountain; and there
She fed us to her scabied brood, screaming for
Our sweet flesh to sour their appetite still;
Slithering free from her craw, I escaped to tell.

Three Stories Misheard From One: A Younger Worm Tries To Recount What Graybeard Has Just Said

1

Truth's answers to the sea:

                The leap of calm bathers, bread,

Ice;

    the dying suite of disciples;

                  they ar-

Rived, the textures of seasons;

                   the naves of leaves are your bed;

Winter skies plant seeds that please the early star;

The waves invent love.

2

            Moonlight on the marsh,

Ended, flame-fled for love; "Defend Princess Waterfall,"

I heard him; as his feeling broke, heart

Thrashed in shudders, leavened; flesh, then the wind curled

About him; like a beaten horse, rain came, then it snowed.

3

The sea, borealis to the gusting zephyr,

Was once a caliph who, in his sea-kissed moment, adored

The forests of escaping moons strumming fire;

Assuaged for this, their shouts enraptured the tide pools;

Sea, liven in freedom, carry comfort to these tales.

Starfish Song: The Biologist Doctor Gwilliam, After Years In His Laboratory

He walks into the night stillness; his students

Are gone; in the west are constellations

He hasn't seen before, a dampness

He has never felt, the scent of a different ocean;

All the next day he looks at his planet;

"My love for you is always, like water, total,

Submerging," he whispers, "like an alphabet

I've only now learned to read"; in a tide pool

A hermit crab purrs; a sea anemone

Flowers; in the second millennium

Of the Moisture reign, a starfish, like memory,

Sings to the peaceful, the sleeping Doctor Gwilliam;

Sea horses play on their seaweed guitars

Of how we will all rise, like water, toward the stars.

What The Leech Oracle Prophesies:
The Fate Of These Tapestries

Against my will she electrifies — through the socket

She sucks my blood with — this sense of my work's fate;

Now it flows, commingles, my blunt, sapped heart

Heavy with it; to find the fall or flight

Of the silks my skill weaves, the leech enters

My ivory gates to read, to rend my heart's blood:

"What will be found," she says, "is a fragment you've never

Witnessed or imagined; and only its pieces will stand —

See, I hold them toward you: 'the wave crests illumine

Galileo Dolphin, a leaping star...; then, turning

His dream antenna towards her... Doctor Gwilliam...;

His love for her...; arrival of burning...,

The Duchess...; their moonlight sin, the slain...

Troops... she...; then the rolling clouds flame...'"

How The Wolf Became King: The Aged Genii Continues His Tale

A wolf gazed at the bloodied city of grape

When its gates opened, and genies jumped from the seedlings

Onto his back; after fighting the bees with his cape

Of honey, after hiding from the stars' hiss, sacking

The mountains of daggers braised by Moonlight, who lured

Him to the Dolphin Queen in her Citadeled

Castle of pearl, the wolf grew powerful

As a king; draped in human skins he ruled

In pity; with a beast's heart and a beast's pride

He ruled with magic; he swam into the air

And brought back breath; he found Death's city in the underside

Of grass and roots, and he smuggled your sleep; from there

He faintly heard, like the ghost of a rose in its frost,

What Love had once done, and at what cost.

The Story of Humans, What Love Did For Them, And Where Their Language Came From: The Aged Genii Tells What It Was The Wolf King Says He Heard

Between the damp sheets in the lairs of humans,
In their unearthly cities when they were most
Like us, Love longed for these silent Calibans;
She rose towards them through the nebulaic frosts
Of her loneliness; with the strands of her body's sap
She spun for them mutations of desire,
Unravelings they barely understood, a map
That glimmered with the pathways of her fire;

When, stumbling, they followed, their words flowered;
Thus began their journeys of touch; like the wolves
On the moon hills and the whales on the wave cliffs who clamored
In tongues through which we sculpted shapes called selves,
They gathered in language; they began to glow,
Glistening with words, through which they came to know.

A Reminiscence Of Early Loves: Why Moonlight Moves Across The Sky

Duchess: That long, still-sweetening memory: As my army defined
Itself and gathered round me mottled and sieve-
Like as a mackerel sky, I took you to my castle, mine;
I led you…; my archers womanned the walls, my slaves
The elves sang, as you touched the folds of my skin; oh,
All this I remember now like yesterday…

Moonlight: I loved you, when I first saw you through the bowed
Branches as you slept and I thought, "just to lay
Alongside you!" I loved the way your skin scent,
Like ferns in the summer forest, soothed my shrill
Voices, urging, uncommitted; so I went,
I go, among night skies looking for the will

To stop, rest; I felt that in your arms.
Duchess: So come, love, come, and let me kiss away your storms.

More From Her Autobiography: The Duchess of Moisture Tells How She Fell In Love With And Grew To Hate Moonlight

I couldn't stand my love loving someone

Other than me; I can't unfasten the stays

Of my love, my burning for this anti-sun;

I can't for all my tide's longing;

                                 O, the ways

Of Moonlight! I remember when I let

The lambent seashore sigh of us rise — sing

Your dirge of desire, Weaver; my wet

Body stroked by him, I loved, in the swaying

Concupiscence of rain, as my return; how

Could you know such sweetness? He lay me down and kissed

The slit that rings my thighs — how could you know,

Weaver, hidden by morning, my summoned mist,

His entering — how could you know the first time?

Well, I'm not some schoolyard whore; he is mine.

Why, When Some See Beauty, Some Don't: Monkey Boy And The Fox

Like I give Felisha grubs in a Kleenex,

Like at lunch I play solos, and these sheep people

Say, "Where's your guitar?" They don't even realize Hendrix;

Like I point where I sit in this sunlight pool

And they say, "Yeah"; man, like it's weird in nighttime,

Felisha's father comes, and I'm in this tree,

Watching his daughter undress in the comforts of home;

Like it's different in jungles — flowers will be

Spring crazy, and animals want each other

And they just do it; like on my motorcycle

My arm hangs, scrapes the yellow line, and there's

These sparks and this beauty, man; 'cause bloody knuckles

Plowing concrete for Hendrix's vision, *my* foxy lady,

Don't mean nothing when you're making beauty.

Part Three:
Tales From The Citadel Of Pearl
(The Tapestries Of Wishing)

Where I Write Down What I Understand Of The Woodcutter Who Has Turned Into A Tree

Regrets? No. In my hair the bright birds choir,
Flowers float midst my lichened bark; my heart
Lives there, its helve honed here; am I a shire
For the wasp? A limbate to the ivy's art?
To everything, yes; what hops through my domed
Canopy? Caterpillar, come, what have you to fear?

Once I man-slept under trees that bloomed;
Their branches braided the moon; then ants reared
Me through the crackling leaves; when I settled
Into the soft, damp earth, worms wove the caul
They wrapped me in; I think my speech seems addled
To you, a hiss of a burning sapling; fall,
And my leaves blush to the sun's light; like wands
My branches wave in these sweet, last summer winds.

Late In The Year: Where I Still Try To Understand The Woodcutter Tree

Now it's winter; snow comes like the dreamed
Offal in the woods' death-farm; O, in these mists
It's not far to learn a truth, then find it damned;
Haven't you seen like whisperings in drifts
Of leaves broken by wind? The sadnesses
Of trees ghost through me; I dreamed in the cloudy morning
Hummingbirds rose, and I ached for my soft flesh
Shriven in moonlight to be with them; moaning
Is what I do best you see; in my high limbs
I fairly creak with it when night blows;
But of Moonlight you've asked, who came here once, what of him,
And the Duchess — how her black hatred flowered,
As he spurred away in his love for the Waterfall —
So you've asked me, so I'll tell you all.

The Tapestry Of Shame: The Woodcutter Tree Tells How Moonlight Left Princess Waterfall

I saw Moonlight command his chariot's
Team of gilded bears before the morning;
Rains had turned the forests into chamber pots
That overflowed; torrents loosened my mooring
In the dirt as the bears pawed where clouds curled,
As Moonlight knelt beside me; mired in worms,
Gnawed on in my crypt of roots, burled,
Bathed in mites, I felt ashamed, but the storms
Had gathered; I was "convenient," he said;
"Princess, Love, stay here," in rushes of wind
I heard him; when the soldiers came he fled;
They rooted me down to my blood-sapped rind;
My syrup dripped into the earth from my wounds;
Then a spring flowed from my roots like so many words.

What I Hear In The Creek Stones:
The Princess Waterfall's Song

Shall I go to the water   by the swift water
Yes if it flows to you by the Woodcutter Tree I grieve
Listen the sea is he chained too by desire

Betrayed by shadows did soldiers let you live
Along that road along that road you travel
In the dream grass dream thighs move and we come

If in ten years you find this in that deepened hill
Know this my love know this one night there was a dream
One night I saw a light know this my love know this

I watched its brightness I climbed the Woodcutter Tree
Overjoyed I watched for you in the branches
I thought you had returned would you still find me pretty

I saved myself for you but it was not you
I wanted to run to you but it was not you

Why We Get What We Can Get: Monkey Boy Hangs Out With The Squirrels

Like Mr. Buck says I'm suspended; Right;
Like Felisha, I saw you peel down, Friday,
Near the woodshop, after the game that night;

You didn't know me; I thought, "Infidelity,
Man, she's done it to me"; I wanted it
Good just once, Felisha; like in the trees, squirrel
Junkies on needle-thin branches shoot
Up and up; then they leap, their tails in a whirl;

Like, it was like a beast was climbing my baby;
Like, a hand like an otter slid down your hair;
A puma pawed what should have been saved for me;
You lifted, skirt like a skunk's tail; you didn't scare;

But I did; when you squealed, as you came, I let go,
Jumped, pretending, that to meet me, your hips rose.

The Tapestry Of Distances: Where I Ride On Hawk's Back

Up here my jaws grit in this cold — Whoosh!
This wind winnows away warmth; I've a whim
For whispering dark leaves; Hawk, whoa! I wish
My swooped, roller coaster stomach would... Wham!
Now Hawk totes his conked mouse like a lunch pail
To his aerie near the sea; I'm borne on wingtips spread
Toward horizons and sun flames; we peel
Through the soft silks of sky's cocoon; the world grows red;

The vantage from where we look is called "perspective";
So, instead of down there, can I, in air
Up here, embrace more with my "insect" love?
How much can I truly love from afar?

I'd rather be down there and close to you;
To be ever closer, that's *my* point of view.

The Tapestry Of Consequence: Princess Waterfall Seduces Moonlit Lake, Now A Young Girl, And Possum Hears The Elves Enchained In The World Below

Nights when we animals drank from her, the Princess
Missed Moonlight most; finally, when winter had blown
Away, and stream beds rang raiments of praises
In the water rush where mountain flowers bloom,
The Princess knelt, her daughter scented in sleep:

"My love   place your body's solace here
Around me water quickens   it draws me deep
Into your sweetness   into the tangled hair
Of evening   let us sleep now," she whispered;

Enchained elves anviled warnings from their darkness:
"The Duchess wants   wants   wants no wish spared
Black torrential rains want the child   The Duchess
Wants   Wants. . ."; thus Possum, Old Ear-in-the-Ground,
Made out the boned world below, as it cracked, groaned.

Separate Soliloquies: Where I Have Premonitions Of Moonlit Lake's Fate, As Far Away The Duchess Of Moisture Finds Her Sleeping In The Woods

Myself: You seemed my best self   as in wonder I watched you

Duchess: As you bloom   Moonlit Lake   like a spring
                The spirits of snow melt upon you

Myself: In those lengthening days that seasons bring
                Beautiful pale longings   my whispering angels
                Speak to me

Duchess: A wood is an evil world
                Didn't they tell you   it's

Myself: In this ache   chills
                Char my prophesying heart

Duchess: like a wound
                It beguiles even the sweetest rose
                Like you   innocent one

Myself: Moonlit Lake

Duchess: The lusts of soldiers will swarm beyond the sunrise
                For you   innocent one   for you

Myself: Moonlit Lake!

Duchess: Though none of us could choose from whose
                        loins we came,

          It's the one with power, me, who assigns the blame.

The Tapestry Of Wishing: How The Duchess Of Moisture's Revenge Against Moonlight And Those Closest To Him Began

First, a frost on the spirit — rage stirring, flower
Felt; then coyly, like placid volcanic ash,
Snow fell; then the wind's sea-salt fervor
Began; ice swathed bit by bit like a lash
Unleashed upon us; pulled from me my wishes'
Savaged forms scattered; Duchess revenge
Sent them scouring through the night like witches
Before they fell like a meteor's red-edged
Embers into the sea; now wending their way,
Caravanned by — whom? currents? scaled or scalloped
Harbingers? — I don't know, but far away,
To the Dolphins' Pearl Citadel, they escaped,
And so moved was the queen there that her strong
Magic was stirred; she felt our hurt, you see, our wrong.

Turtle Story: Turtle Tells How He Ferried Caterpillar To The Dolphin Queen

Yes, I am the crinkly faced, or worse; dumb-
Ness seems to steal upon me, true, but content?
I am; many-legged weaver full of wisdom,
Don't fear; think of me a kindly continent;

Come on, climb that reed until your weight
Bends it like a bow and, like forgiveness,
Touches me; I love the reeds that sway like wheat;
That's it; hug my shell now; the fog rises —
We should go, it's best you don't be seen
You know; fog like shells all made of quiet;

No one laughs at me here, and my Queen..., my Queen
Must always remain Duchess concealed; see that quaint
Crab who scuttles about like a traipsing skull?

A spy, sifting for her through seas, ancient, tropical.

Two Characters In Search Of A Fairy Tale — Divergent Longings Near A Volcanic Island: Where Turtle Becomes Homesick, While Caterpillar Longs To Live In The Sea

Turtle	Caterpillar
This fiery coralled island,	Like a starlit sombrero,
These waters strumming	Like sunsets that sambaed
Into themselves	landwards where some bear all
Of their thirst	Of their bodies like the sun's bread
Rising into the light	Passing through the mouth of want,
Through a mist of hunger	Until it stills in its hush
Of where, what you've just been,	Like a present you can't
Have lived through, have known,	Have seen, in the inrush
Of desire washing it away,	That the sea instills;
Which won't let go;	Into your heart it comes;

A loom of longing weaves your life,	It fills
What you've always known:	These places that are our homes;
Those sea-salt roses:	These starlit waters at peace:
What is most true,	Show us; and our false longings will cease.

The Dolphin Queen: Turtle And Caterpillar Enter The Citadel Of Pearl, Only To Find The Duchess Has Been There First

Turtle: These red tides I labor through —
Caterpillar: Thick as blood

Turtle: Colored like welts
Caterpillar: Something makes the salt air ill

Turtle: This brined sea wind tastes bitter to me
Caterpillar: Biled

Turtle: My breath comes hard
Caterpillar: So close to the citadel

Turtle: This all seems wrong
Caterpillar: Is there no welcoming

Turtle: No whale song
Caterpillar: No starred parapets like mountains

Turtle: No Queen's Guards
Caterpillar: From where crowds wave   flags winnowing

Turtle: Here are no subjects
Caterpillar: Only verbed motions

Turtle:	The wind-shalloped waves
Caterpillar:	Tug me to this bay
Turtle:	In which nothing lives
Caterpillar:	In the dead-jammed canal
Turtle:	By the Pearl Castle
Caterpillar:	The dead float like buoys
Turtle:	Beside their Queen
Caterpillar:	Slain in the gutted coral
Turtle:	The Moisture Duchess
Caterpillar:	Who thinks through violence
Turtle:	Rules only these spelless nights now
Caterpillar:	Ruined voiceless

The Duchess of Moisture's Revenge: The Murder Of Princess Waterfall's Daughter

Now Boom! Boom of brain bursting,
                                    bone fright,
Barracuda troops bristling;
                                    life energy
Lanced, banged through her.
                                    Face-pulped. Wish-flight.
To them, she wasn't "child," she was "enemy."

Oh, God, I watched her.
                                    Now, like the murmuring dream
Waters, past the snowy egret, his lullaby
Sighs of white feathers,
                                    her spirit sidles through green
Pond meadows, through tide pools,
                                    into the sea.

Mists now like phantoms pass through what I weave;
        Like shimmering-gowned heart clenching, these drifts
Through the brackish inlet:
                                    Is this how desire leaves?
God, I'm shivering cold in these dream drafts.

Child, I dreamt Waterfall met the sea — there was light,
Incandescent union — it wasn't too late.

The Duchess's Destruction Of Earth's 999 Moons: Her Account Of Recent Events, Both On And Off The Record

"You'll know my pain by how much pain I cause,
And still my heart forever will hurt more."
— from The Duchess of Moisture's Autobiography

I have loved, Weaver, as much as anyone could;
And I long, I have longed, the length of milky time,
But my breasts, my heart invaded, were then made cold;
Tell them, too, that in youth my heart would teem
With the blown breath of Moonlight's April rain —
I was a young girl then; I was...; My words
Metamorphose to mist reminiscing pain;

When Moonlight rose from me into the woods
I culled among my troops my curdling hate
For her, young girl whom Moonlight prizes most;
Thus, a broken heart for a broken heart;
Let them pine forever; those nights, my flood hosts
Of eroding tears cankered the moons — my plaint —
Until all   but the strongest   like me   split apart.

Written In Her Old Age: The Princess Waterfall's Other Song

I was lost   sparrows led me home

A dry August   tears ran their course

Farthest love   for you   I could not see the moon

My farthest love   words become a kiss

Will it take a thousand years   these candles

Remember me   these breaths we share

In the rings waters make   by the bridge to night's castle

In the chevelure of stones   under mountain stars

Stay   kiss me   the sun sets   so still I leave my body

As a dream beyond my bones   is it so wrong

Love   make me feel   to want so badly

Lover filled with lover   as an unending song

O young girl of memory   a body bathed in sweat

Come to me   ravenous with kisses sweet

Part Four:
Tales Of Ever After
(The Tapestries Of Ending
And Never Ending)

Withdrawals: Monkey Boy, Wandering The Forest Waiting For The Angels, Tells Of His Death Moment

Like blood bathing me, like Angel's lips,
Like Felicia's; like little mites scour,
Scrape my brain skin — I smell mint when they stop;

Like there's this ground bone marrow-like powder
And somehow I snort it in like coke, and I'm laved
In perfume, like holy water, like...,

$\qquad\qquad\qquad\qquad$ like a ghost
Pompoming cunt and cock, if not for a loved
Heart, feels nothing — I saw that in these lost
Visions after I hit the cool concrete;

$\qquad\qquad\qquad\qquad$ toked-
On like a joint, my soul seems sucked-out
Into a teary bead, like when that joke
Of a teacher showed how a sperm dances about
An egg;

$\qquad$ I want, so badly, my life back —
It's like cigarettes burning regret into heartbreak.

On The Origins Of Rainbows: Where Moonlight Grants Me An Interview

"Inspired the fireflies," that's what they said, when the war
Started, and that I raised tides to the barricades
When the Duchess came, and that meteors bore
Down from my eyes, and that barracudas
Of moisture attacked and the winds of galaxies
Surged through my hair, and that I led the brunt
Of the beaten moth armies — all good as lies;

What is true: When the battles began, I hid in a burnt-
Out snake lair, grew small as a sliver; yes,
I was caught, then escaped far away; I've sent postcards
To show that; and I loved and still bless the Princess
Waterfall; I gave her the rainbow that guards
Her; I'm tired now; under the crackling leaves
I'm a shadow's shadow; the others? Let them believe.

Graduation Ceremony: Monkey Boy, In Heaven Now, Learns To Be An Angel

Like they give me wings as red as my cuts,

And icy, like they give to penitents; like on the dusty field

Near those hills, where I trained in their Quonset huts,

I'm flying; like when the windsock is unfurled,

Stiffened by winds of the weeping, I'm gone; like I strike

Down spiraling into the suicides' anger;

Like in their sobbing wards I'm diving like a shrike

Into their salty wounds; outside, always after

More, the Duchess, with her dizzying, freezing rains

And her worms and toads, attacks through the mist —

Fuck it; like I'm kissing the cut wrists and the burns

On the suicides' arms; like I'm giving them blood as kissed

As Christ's; like I'm bending over them as they sleep,

And I'm whispering, like in dreams; like they hear me.

The Tapestry Of Hesitation: What Frog Says When, His Quest Ended, He Reaches The Sea

Moist from the weeping in my bones, and so
Ever more like the sea, mourning the sea's
Shored caesura sliding away, this I know:
That if I could make the sea lie still and touch me,
I would; why then do I think back to you,
My love, in our pond-bottomed bed of mud and loam?

Ocean of oceans, in your inundating blue-
Sea dreams of water, could I be more alone
Than here, where bird songs in the wind-gnarled trees bent
Seaward lift beyond me, where the ocean melts
In runneled light and clouds smudged yellow with sunsets?

I want to drown where quivering love is felt,

Back, in the loin swells of your hips, the becalmed
Bay behind us, where I become lost in you, where I became.

When Penance Comes: Monkey Boy Talks To The Near-Suicide

It's like Angels made daybreak in my heart;
Like I'm a gift for you, like a wish or something,
And now I'm looking at you, consumed by the part
That blooms music; it's like soaring;
Like now I'm feeling through the front of your nightgown,
And you're all so beautiful; like under
A school desk, someone's carved your initials down
Deep beside her own; like at a mirror,
Someone is combing her hair for you; like someone
Fantasizing you just to feel how close
She can breathe you near; like I've seen it done,
Someone pinning themselves with a love-starved rose
To brush you by in the halls — so much you don't know;
Don't die; like, it's alright; I'm here, shh, now.

Why Memory Grows Fonder The Farther You Go: Where I Find Scraps Of Postcards Sent From Moonlight When He Escaped To The Universe's Edge

"Ground fog curling through the violets… moles,
Or somethings, live under the barn… in the flower
Bed, beaver trails? Teach me my way, birdcalls…
Ringing from down in the village… is the water
Leaving secrets? On the porch it taps messages…
In the dialogue my eyes have with the fragrant
Clouds, I hear the fields stretch toward their edges…
Did hornets live in the eaves? I forget,
But I'm sure of the fat spiders near the back steps…
One sips the evening here like a light sauterne…
You see so much at the Universe's edge; sunsets
Shift on various ridges of the mountain…
Its night's first shadow slow dances with the sun…
Their bodies so close, they seem almost as one…"

The Tapestry Of Leaves: What I Read When I Chance To Find Three Unfinished Journal Entries, Early Drafts From The Duchess Of Moisture's Autobiography

I

"I smell the sea — it's like a burning passion
In my heart; at the center of my soul's passion?
Moonlight — at the center of all I am;
I've not absolved any of you from pain."

II

                                      "'Shines
In prose,… writes in the black ink of felt life,'
My critics will say; and then, 'But she loosened blood
Onto the world';
                I say to them now: 'what I left
Is but testimony to how his sin bloomed
In me, to how lost longing bleeds in me alone — me!'"

III

"Tonight I wish I felt the burly desire
Of prayer, for before his absence ruled my destiny,
Before the fasts of my flesh turned into hunger,
I was innocent as you; now my world swims on fire;
I've not the heart to fan it on, or blow it out anymore."

The Tapestry Of Images: The Duchess Of Moisture Sighing To Herself As She Looks At Her Reflection In The Pond

Under the moon we kissed, where the star trails thin, float
    Under the moon, under the moon of sorrow;

Under the full moon, tethered by our hearts' fate,
I crept under the moon, under the moon of sorrow;

    Under the full moon you pulled me down upon you;
    Under the moon, it was under the moon of sorrow

    You entered me, my thighs rose petals moist with dew
    Under the moon, under the moon of my sorrow;

Under the full moon my watery bones,
Motionless, shorn of loving you again,

    And my anger, like a knife slit in the throat that shone
    Blood stained and still in the waning light, sunk in pain;

I didn't care what would come tomorrow,
    Under the moon, under the moon of sorrow.

The Earth As Scheherazade:
The Biologist's Lecture

The earth, my dears, is a book to read, as lit-
Eral in its "realness" as a human's bible,
Or your hearts, for there are many books that transmit
Truths, and you must learn to read them all;
Look at the book of earth: Its fossil narratives
Collide, coincide, lose themselves, pick up
Again, such stories of different characters' lives,
Evolving, transmuting — who'd ever wish them to stop?

In the end we're all just tapestries, my dears,
Our lives as interthreaded as our voices;
Who can say one wholly disappears
When our warped, beaten threads unravel,

and our shed pieces

Shuttle to a larger loom, as we weave,
Never aparting, even as we leave.

The Final Tapestry: To Be Read After My Death

Over the pools that make one forgetful,

My life will burn in the goings of seasons;

Forest memories will become things useful,

My life; I will be given robes and crowns,

My life's ending; I will lust for hunger,

My life; I will rise on the wind; like a bride,

Evening's rose hush before starlight, before

My memory of childhood and bread,

Will undress me, and my female beauty will stay;

My life, that transient part that wants to remain,

Will end, as the night will tell a story;

It will start: "As it has always begun,

Your ending will begin in the thin shell

Of departure with a peck of light; you'll feel…"

Final Words: Where I Take Notes On My Execution

The thorny spears of the rose rage from all sides;
Toad soldiers rouse me from the dandelion;
Now the nightmare mire of the pollywog, the insides
Of the pond bottom; mud of centuries my dungeon;

The Duchess pronounces my sentence as she floats;
I think, "this one will stay mine"; my dead father
Has become a frog I dream; "I know you," he croaks;
The pond mist settles; I need his caress here,
See where I'm hurt? Toad breathing near nightfall — no moon
Will come now; parachute throats, colors of helmets;
This tapestry will shroud me by the next noon;
My executioner will come in moments;

His web shivers; a guard's bellow — now the jaws'
Blackness; now the sentence ends; thus I was…

Acknowledgements

Grateful acknowledgement is made to the following publications, in which the poems listed, some of them in slightly different versions, first appeared.

"Each In Their Turn: Forest Creatures At Twilight"; "Final Tapestry: To Be Read After My Death"; "The Tapestry Of Distances: Where I Ride On Hawk's Back"; and "Separate Soliloquies: Where I have Premonitions of Moonlit Lake's Fate, As Far Away The Duchess Of Moisture Finds Her sleeping In The Woods" were first published in *Café Solo*.

"Why, When Some See Beauty, Some Don't: Monkey Boy And The Fox"; "Withdrawals: Monkey Boy, Wandering The Forest Waiting For The Angels, Tells Of His Death Moment"; and "When Penance Comes: Monkey Boy Talks To The Near-Suicide" were first published in *Chicago Review*.

"How, in The Season's First Snowfall, Frog Came To Leave His Pond In Quest Of The Sea" was first published in *The DMQ Review*.

"Where I Write Down What I Understand Of The Woodcutter Who Has Turned Into A Tree" and "Late In The Year: Where I Still Try To Understand The Woodcutter Tree" were first published in *The Dickinson Review*.

"Three Stories Misheard From One: A Younger Worm Tries To Recount What Graybeard Has Just Said"; "The Tapestry Of Shame: The Woodcutter Tree Tells How Moonlight Left Princess Waterfall"; "What I Hear In The Creek Stones: The Princess Waterfall's Song"; "The Tapestry Of Consequence: Princess Waterfall Seduces Moonlit Lake, Now A Young Girl, And Possum Hears The Elves Enchained In The World Below"; "The Duchess of Moisture's Revenge: The Murder Of Princess Waterfall's Daughter"; and "Written In Her Old Age: The Princess Waterfall's Other Song" were first published in *ForPoetry.Com*.

"The Tapestry Of Hesitation: What Frog Says When, His Quest Ended, He Reaches The Sea" was first published in *Larry's Poetry Review*.

"Tapestry Of Blossoming Senses: A Notation Of Spring While Watching Two Bicyclists Stop By A Pond" was first published in *m.a.g.*

"On The Origins Of Rainbows: Where Moonlight Grants Me An Interview" was first published in *The Missouri Review*.

"Introductory Notes"; "The Breeze-Fluttered Tapestry: April"; "The Antagonists: The Duchess Of Moisture, The Empress Of Waterfowl"; "When The Grape Became Purple: The Aged Genii Recalls The War Of His Kind Against The Moisture Duchess"; "Why We Sometimes Don't Say Anything In Dreams: Monkey

Boy"; "The Duchess Of Moisture Reads To Me From Her Autobiography, The Early Years"; "Monkey Boy's In-Class English Theme: Angel and a Desperado Heart"; "Angel's Passion: Angel And Monkey Boy Park Off The Deep Woods Road"; "Where I Comment Upon The Main Action In These Tapestries So Far"; "Starfish Song: The Biologist Doctor Gwilliam, After Years In His Laboratory"; "What The Leech Oracle Prophesies: The Fate Of These Tapestries"; "A Reminiscence Of Early Loves: Why Moonlight Moves Across the Sky"; "More From Her Autobiography: The Duchess Of Moisture Tells How She Fell In Love With And Grew To Hate Moonlight"; "Why We Get What We Can Get: Monkey Boy Hangs Out With The Squirrels"; "The Tapestry Of Wishing: How The Duchess Of Moisture's Revenge Against Moonlight And Those Closest To Him Began"; "Turtle Story: Turtle Tells How He Ferried Caterpillar To The Dolphin Queen"; "The Dolphin Queen: Turtle And Caterpillar Enter The Citadel Of Pearl, Only To Find The Duchess Has Been There First"; "The Duchess's Destruction Of Earth's 999 Moons: Her Account Of Recent Events, Both On And Off the Record"; "Graduation Ceremony: Monkey Boy, In Heaven Now, Learns To Be An Angel"; "Why Memory Grows Fonder The Farther You Go: Where I Find Scraps Of Postcards Sent From Moonlight When He Escaped To The Universe's Edge"; "The Tapestry Of Leaves: What I Read When I Chance To Find Three Unfinished Journal Entries, Early Drafts From The Duchess Of Moisture's Autobiography"; "The Tapestry Of Images: The Duchess Of Moisture Sighing To Herself As She

Looks At Her Reflection In The Pond"; and "Final Words: Where I Take Notes On My Execution" were first published in *Mudlark: An Electronic Journal of Poetry & Poetics*.

"The Earth As Scheherazade: The Biologist's Lecture"; "Where Lullabies Go: The Pond On An Early Winter Evening"; "Two Characters In Search Of A Fairy Tale — Divergent Longings Near A Volcanic Island: Where Turtle Becomes Homesick, While Caterpillar Longs To Live In The Sea"; "How The Wolf Became King: The Aged Genii Continues His Tale," and "The Story of Humans, What Love Did For Them, And Where Their Language Came From: The Aged Genii Tells What It Was The Wolf King Says He Heard" were first published in *The National Poetry Review*.

"At The Worm's Campfire: The Graybeard's Story" was first published in *Onthebus*.

Biography:

S.D. Lishan is an Associate Professor of English at The Ohio State University, where he teaches courses in creative writing, poetry, critical writing, and the literature of the fantastic. His poems, fiction, and creative nonfiction have appeared in the *Bellingham Review, Xconnect, Barrow Street, Creative Nonfiction, Brevity, Bellingham Review, ForPoetry.com, Kenyon Review, The National Poetry Review, The American Poetry Journal, In Possse Review, Mudlark, Arts & Letters, New England Review, Versedaily* and others. He also writes lyrics for songwriter, Andrea Perry. Her third CD, *River of Stars*, containing a number of their collaborations, will appear in the autumn, 2006. He has just completed a new volume of poems, and, as of this writing, he is currently in the final revision stages of a novel entitled *Lightseed*.

www.ingramcontent.com/pod-product-compliance
Lightning Source LLC
Chambersburg PA
CBHW022030090426
42739CB00006BA/364